Tiny Triumphs

The Power of Micro Steps in Achieving Continuous Improvement

T.D Errol

"Tiny Triumphs: The Power of Micro Steps in Achieving Continuous Improvement"

Tiny Triumphs

The Power of Micro Steps in Achieving Continuous Improvement

By
T.D. Errol

"Tiny Triumphs: The Power of Micro Steps in Achieving Continuous Improvement"

Copyright © 2024 by T.D. Errol.

All rights reserved. No part of this book may be used or reproduced without written permission except for brief quotations in critical articles or reviews.
Printed in the United States of America.

For more information,
contact:

T.D Errol

Email: errolpublishing@gmail.com

Book design by T.D. Errol
Cover design by T.D. Errol

ISBN: 9798325923425
Imprint: Independently published

Share Your Thoughts with Us!

I hope you enjoyed reading my book. Your insights and experiences mean the world to me. I'd like to hear your thoughts on whether the story resonated with you or if any area could be improved.

Please consider leaving a review on Amazon or the platform where you purchased. Your feedback helps me grow as an author and guides fellow readers in their choices.

Alternatively, feel free to email me personally at errolpublishing@gmail.com. Every word you share contributes to the story's evolving journey.

Thank you for being a cherished part of this adventure.

Warm regards,

T.D. Errol

Bio

T.D. Errol, a Colorado-based author and business strategist, boasts a diverse background, from serving with the United States Marine Corps to pivotal leadership roles in the corporate world. Beyond his professional accolades, T.D. transformed personal adversities into opportunities, notably harnessing the mindful art of intentional walking after significant back surgery. Marrying military insights with rich managerial experiences, he offers a treasure trove of wisdom in leadership, strategy, and personal growth. Through captivating narratives, T.D. champions the essence of mindful evolution in both personal and professional spheres.

Other Books From T.D. Errol

Think Smart: Mastering Problem Solving and Critical Thinking for Professional Success

The Power of Checklists: Mastering Momentum for Business Success

The Evolving Self: Mastering Continuous Improvement in the Prime of Life

Mastering Knowledge in the Digital Age: A Young Professional's Guide to PKM

Decisive Choices: Mastering Strategies for Effective Decision Making and Problem Solving

Embracing Change and Adapting: The importance of being open to change and adapting to new situations or environments as part of personal growth.

Building Emotional Intelligence: Enhancing Personal and Professional Relationships

Forward

A world that often glorifies the grandiose and the instantaneous, it is easy to overlook the profound impact of the small and the gradual. Yet, the seeds of substantial change are sown in these tiny, consistent steps. "Tiny Triumphs: The Power of Micro Steps in Achieving Continuous Improvement" is a testament to the transformative power of micro steps, an ancient and urgently relevant concept.

This book is based on the observation that real, lasting change comes not from sporadic leaps but from deliberate, incremental progress. Whether in personal development, business, health, or relationships, continuous improvement through micro-steps invites us to rethink our approach to goals and challenges. It offers a more sustainable path to success, marked not by occasional bursts of effort but by persistence and regularity.

As you turn these pages, you will discover stories of individuals and organizations that have embraced this philosophy, achieving remarkable outcomes not through overwhelming force or revolutionary innovations but through simple, persistent movement forward. These narratives are not just instructive; they are a call to action.

Moreover, this book provides practical frameworks and strategies anyone can incorporate daily. With these tools, the journey of a thousand miles begins with a single, manageable step — and then another.

"Tiny Triumphs" is more than just a guide; it is an invitation to view your life and work through a different lens, where the minor actions are accorded the importance they deserve. It challenges the myth that only big leaps count and celebrates the subtle art of making a little go a long way.

Welcome to a world of incremental change, where every small step is a victory. Welcome to "Tiny Triumphs."

Contents

Introduction: The Art of Small Beginnings — 11

Part I: The Foundations of Micro Steps

Chapter 1: Understanding Micro Steps — 15

Chapter 2: Cultivating a Micro Steps Mindset — 19

Chapter 3: Setting Yourself Up for Success — 24

Part II: Applying Micro Steps in Various Aspects of Life

Chapter 4: Personal Growth and Development — 30

Chapter 5: Professional and Career Development — 37

Chapter 6: Financial Well-being — 41

Part III: Overcoming Obstacles with Micro Steps

Chapter 7: Facing Challenges Head-on — 47

Chapter 8: Adapting and Adjusting Strategies — 51

Chapter 9: Maintaining Momentum — 56

Chapter 10: From Micro Steps to Macro Leaps — 60

Conclusion — 67

Appendices — 73

Introduction:
The Art of Small Beginnings

In our quest for success and self-improvement, we often envision change as a dramatic, sweeping transformation—a personal revolution that upends habits and overhauls routines overnight. Yet, such radical shifts are seldom sustainable. The true path to lasting progress is less glamorous but significantly more effective: it involves embracing the power of micro steps. These small, incremental changes might seem trivial in isolation but culminating in profound, lasting improvements.

This approach taps into the enduring power of consistency and the transformative potential of modest efforts. It adheres to the philosophy that significant changes come from small beginnings. It is grounded in the understanding that every monumental journey begins with a modest step. Rather than daunting leaps, small, deliberate actions pave the way to meaningful achievement.

The Principle of Incremental Change

At the core of micro steps lies a fundamental truth about human behavior: the smaller the step, the easier it is to take. This is crucial because the most challenging part of any task is often just getting started. When goals are broken down into smaller, more manageable pieces, they become less intimidating and more attainable. This method not only eases the initiation of tasks but also helps sustain momentum. Each small step completed reinforces the next, creating a positive cycle that builds confidence and fosters further action.

For example, a goal as simple as becoming more organized can start with decluttering a single drawer rather than overhauling an entire office. This single act is a micro step; it's manageable and immediately rewarding, which motivates further action—a principle that can be applied to almost any area of life.

Historical Roots in Kaizen

The philosophy behind micro steps is not new. It echoes the principles of Kaizen, which originated in Japan during the post-World War II era. Initially applied to improve manufacturing processes, Kaizen—which translates to "continuous improvement"—is based on the idea that small, ongoing positive changes can reap significant improvements. Over the decades, Kaizen has transcended its industrial origins to influence areas as diverse as healthcare, business management, and personal development.

Adopting Kaizen in everyday life means viewing each day as an opportunity to improve just a little bit. It's about embracing change incrementally and celebrating small victories along the way. This approach is efficient because it integrates change into daily life without the overwhelm often accompanying more significant initiatives.

Micro Steps in Personal and Professional Development

In personal and professional development, micro steps provide a practical methodology for self-improvement. They encourage a mindset that values persistence in small doses and continuous, mindful effort rather than sporadic bursts of exertion. In personal development, this could translate into reading a page of a self-help book each night or walking an extra thousand steps daily. Professionally, it might involve improving a work-related skill through regular, short practice sessions instead of waiting for a lengthy seminar.

This incremental approach also offers the flexibility to adjust with minimal disruption. When strategies or efforts are broken down into smaller segments, it's easier to tweak or refine them based on ongoing feedback or changing circumstances. This adaptability is crucial in today's fast-paced world, where conditions and needs can change rapidly.

Looking Ahead

As we delve deeper into the concept of micro steps throughout this book, we will explore their application across various dimensions of life—from enhancing personal health and wellness to advancing career goals and enriching relationships. Each chapter will offer actionable insights and real-world examples of how small steps can lead to significant changes, demonstrating that continuous improvement is not just a business strategy but a personal one.

This introduction to the subtle yet powerful philosophy of micro steps aims to inform and inspire. It invites readers to reconsider their approach to personal and professional development. By understanding and implementing the principles of incremental change and Kaizen, we can all learn to appreciate that the minor steps often lead to the most significant rewards and that we find the path to true transformation by accumulating tiny, consistent efforts.

Part I:
The Foundations of Micro Steps

Chapter 1:
Understanding Micro Steps

> "Great things are not done by impulse, but by a series of small things brought together." — Vincent Van Gogh.

Definition and Principles of Micro Step

As we delve into the fascinating concept of micro steps in "Tiny Triumphs: The Power of Micro Steps in Achieving Continuous Improvement," we must begin with a foundational understanding. This chapter explores micro steps and the principles that guide their effectiveness. It is crucial for anyone looking to make consistent, incremental progress in any area of life.

Micro steps are small, manageable actions or changes that generate significant progress or transformation. Unlike grand, sweeping changes that require substantial effort and can often lead to overwhelming failure, micro steps are minimalistic, almost trivial actions that are easy to implement and maintain. The core idea behind micro steps is that small, consistent changes are more sustainable and effective over time than sporadic, large-scale efforts. This principle taps into the psychological comfort of handling manageable tasks, reducing the intimidation and resistance often associated with significant challenges.

Each small step builds upon the previous, creating a chain of improvements contributing to a larger goal. This underscores the importance of regularity and habit formation in achieving long-term objectives. Given their size, micro steps can be easily adjusted according to feedback and results. This flexibility allows for more personalized and responsive approaches to goals, making it easier to overcome obstacles and plateaus. Just as financial investments grow exponentially due to the power of compounding, micro steps leverage the compound effect of small, repeated efforts. Over time, these tiny changes accumulate substantial benefits.

Micro steps democratize the improvement process by making it accessible to everyone, regardless of resources, skills, or starting points. They propose that improvement is not the exclusive domain of the extraordinarily disciplined or talented but is achievable for anyone who can take a simple step forward. To effectively implement micro steps, begin by defining your overarching goal. Break this goal down into the most minor possible actions. For example, if your goal is to write a book, a micro-step could be as simple as writing one sentence daily. The simplicity of this step makes it psychologically less daunting and practically more feasible, encouraging daily engagement without the stress of facing a massive task.

Micro steps work because they align with human psychology. They reduce fear, minimize procrastination, and simplify tasks to levels that feel 'too easy to fail.' By making each step almost effortless, the resistance to starting is vastly diminished, paving the way for surprising progress. Embracing micro steps means adopting a continuous, incremental, sustainable improvement philosophy. It's about recognizing the power of small actions cumulatively leading to significant changes.

As you incorporate this approach into your personal or professional life, observe how these tiny triumphs accumulate into substantial achievements, embodying the essence of continuous improvement. Stay tuned as we explore how to identify, plan, and execute these micro steps effectively in the upcoming sections.

The science behind small changes: How small actions lead to significant results

Continuing our exploration of micro steps in "Tiny Triumphs: The Power of Micro Steps in Achieving Continuous Improvement," let's delve into the science behind small changes and how these seemingly insignificant actions can produce substantial results.

The science of human behavior and psychological adaptation is at the heart of micro steps' effectiveness. Small changes are powerful because they require minimal psychological energy to initiate. When changes are too significant or daunting, the brain's natural response is resistance, often manifesting as procrastination or avoidance. Micro steps bypass much of this resistance by reducing the scale of change, making it easier to start and maintain new behaviors.

The concept of 'cognitive load,' which refers to the total mental effort used in the working memory, plays a critical role here. More minor actions reduce cognitive load, making tasks seem more manageable and less taxing. This encourages repeated action, which is essential for forming new habits. As these small actions are repeated over time, the brain automatically embeds them into daily routines almost effortlessly.

Neuroplasticity is the brain's ability to reorganize itself by forming new neural connections throughout life. Small, consistent tasks promote strengthening these connections related to new behaviors. Each time a micro-step is performed, it reinforces the neural pathway, making the future performance of the same action smoother and more likely. This is akin to strengthening a muscle through regular exercise; the more the path is used, the stronger it becomes.

Furthermore, the incremental nature of micro steps aligns well with the principle of marginal gains, popularized in fields such as elite sports, where the aggregation of marginal gains suggests that minor improvements in several areas can lead to significant enhancements when combined. In the context of personal development or business, each slight improvement builds on the others but without the overwhelming pressure that comes with trying to make significant leaps at once.

Additionally, the psychological rewards from completing these small steps must be considered. Each completed micro step provides a sense of achievement and progress, which boosts motivation. This is crucial in sustaining long-term changes, as continual rewards reinforce the behavior and encourage persistence. This reward feedback loop is fundamental in behavioral psychology and neuroeconomics, influencing decisions and strengthening the ongoing effort.

Applying micro steps means identifying a desired change or goal and breaking it down into the most minor feasible steps. These steps should be so small that they can be integrated into daily life with minimal disruption. For example, if aiming to improve health, a micro-step could be adding just one vegetable to your dinner plate each night. Over time, these small additions become a natural part of meal preparation and eating habits, contributing to improved health without the resistance and difficulty associated with more drastic diets.

By understanding and utilizing the science behind small changes, you can harness the power of micro steps to create lasting change in any area of your life. It's not just about making change easier; it's about making it stick. As we continue through "Tiny Triumphs," remember that each small step, no matter how insignificant, is a critical component of a more extensive journey toward improvement and success.

Chapter 2:
Cultivating a Micro Steps Mindset

"Patience and perseverance have a magical effect before which difficulties disappear, and obstacles vanish." — John Quincy Adams.

Developing patience and perseverance

As we delve into Chapter 2 of "Tiny Triumphs: The Power of Micro Steps in Achieving Continuous Improvement," we focus on a pivotal aspect: Developing patience and perseverance. This journey is less about monumental leaps and more about embracing the slow, steady progress micro steps offer. Patience and perseverance are not merely virtues to aspire to; they are practical tools that can dramatically enhance your ability to progress toward your goals.

Developing patience is about appreciating the process rather than just pining for the result. It involves understanding that growth happens incrementally and that every small step, no matter how insignificant, is a critical component of larger success. This mindset encourages you to stay the course even when progress feels slow or invisible. Cultivating patience can be challenging in today's fast-paced world, where immediate results are often expected or desired. However, it's crucial to recognize that meaningful change typically requires unfolding time.

Perseverance, on the other hand, is about maintaining your commitment and effort despite challenges and setbacks. The quality helps you progress, even when difficulties or initial enthusiasm wanes. Perseverance is fueled by a clear vision of your goals and the belief that persistent efforts will eventually lead to success. It's about not giving up when the path gets tough and being adaptable in the face of obstacles.

Together, patience and perseverance form a powerful duo. Patience allows you to keep a positive outlook during the gradual journey of improvement, while perseverance provides the grit needed to stick with your plans and overcome hurdles. This combination is essential for anyone looking to adopt a micro-steps mindset because it ensures that you remain engaged and motivated over time, allowing the cumulative effect of small changes to build and eventually manifest as significant transformation.

By nurturing these qualities, you're better equipped to handle the challenges of personal or professional development and set a foundation that fosters continuous improvement. In cultivating a mindset that values patience and perseverance, you prepare yourself to achieve your goals and sustain and build upon those achievements, making every little effort count towards a greater whole.

So, as you proceed with your journey of micro steps, remember that each small, persistent action is a testament to your commitment to long-term success. By embracing patience and perseverance, you'll find that you can navigate the complexities of change with greater ease and confidence, paving the way for a future rich with achievement.

Embracing incremental progress and celebrating small wins

Embracing incremental progress and celebrating small wins are fundamental to maintaining momentum and cultivating a positive mindset toward growth and development. Recognizing and valuing each small achievement creates a rewarding experience that motivates continued effort and builds self-efficacy and confidence.

"Tiny Triumphs: The Power of Micro Steps in Achieving Continuous Improvement"

Embracing incremental progress requires you to shift your perspective from seeking out large, dramatic changes to appreciating the subtler, often overlooked strides you make daily. This shift is pivotal because it aligns your expectations with the reality that most progress in life is gradual and cumulative. It helps to counteract frustration and impatience from not achieving quick results, reinforcing that all progress—no matter its size—is valuable.

Celebrating small wins plays a crucial role in this approach. It acts as positive reinforcement, encouraging you to persist in your efforts. Each time you acknowledge a small success, you reinforce the behavior that led to that success. This boosts your morale and motivates you to continue working towards your goals. Furthermore, celebrating these achievements helps keep your spirits high and your commitment unwavering, especially when larger successes seem distant or elusive.

Moreover, recognizing and celebrating small wins helps build a narrative of success, which is important for your psychological and emotional well-being. It enables you to see yourself as a person who achieves, regardless of the scale of those achievements. This self-perception is crucial for developing resilience and a persistent, positive approach to tackling challenges.

Integrating the practices of embracing incremental progress and celebrating small wins into your routine fosters a resilient, optimistic outlook that propels you towards your goals and makes the journey towards them more enjoyable and fulfilling. Thus, these practices not only aid in achieving goals but also enhance the quality of the experience along the way, making every small step a cause for celebration and a building block for future success.

Overcoming the all-or-nothing mindset

Overcoming the all-or-nothing mindset is critical in fostering a more flexible and forgiving approach to personal and professional development. This mindset often manifests as a rigid, binary way of thinking where activities and efforts are viewed as complete successes or total failures. Such a perspective can be limiting and discouraging, as it leaves little room for the nuanced realities of most human endeavors, where progress often occurs in shades of gray rather than black and white.

To move beyond this restrictive viewpoint, it's important to understand the value of partial successes and the lessons inherent in less-than-perfect outcomes. Recognizing that every effort contributes to learning and growth allows you to see value in every attempt, regardless of its immediate success. This approach reduces the pressure to perform perfectly on every occasion, which can lead to task avoidance or setting unrealistically high standards that stifle progress.

Embracing a mindset that acknowledges the benefits of incremental progress helps dismantle the all-or-nothing approach. By understanding that small steps forward are still moving in the right direction, you can maintain motivation and continue to make efforts that cumulatively lead to significant achievements. This is especially important in complex tasks or long-term projects where progress naturally includes moments of setback or stagnation.

Replacing the all-or-nothing mindset with one that values experimentation and adaptation encourages a more creative and innovative approach to challenges. It allows you to take risks and experiment without fearing failure, as each outcome is seen as an opportunity to learn and adapt. This not only increases your resilience but also enhances your ability to navigate through various situations effectively.

Thus, by overcoming the all-or-nothing mindset, you set the stage for more sustained and consistent progress and cultivate a healthier, more adaptable approach to life's challenges. This helps build a robust foundation for continuous improvement and personal growth, ensuring that each step forward, no matter how small, is valued as a vital part of the journey towards achieving your goals.

Chapter 3:
Setting Yourself Up for Success

"Success is not a random act. It arises from a predictable and powerful set of circumstances and opportunities."

— Malcolm Gladwell

Goal setting for micro steps: Breaking big dreams into actionable steps

Goal setting for micro steps involves breaking big dreams into actionable steps, a strategy that transforms ambitious visions into manageable tasks. This process is crucial because it not only simplifies what might initially appear overwhelming but also sets a clear pathway to achievement that is practical and attainable. By dissecting larger goals into smaller, more digestible components, you increase your chances of success and maintain motivation and focus throughout the journey.

The first step in this method is to define your larger goal clearly. Understanding exactly what you want to achieve provides a solid foundation for the entire process. Once this goal is in place, the next task is identifying the smaller steps that lead incrementally toward this larger objective. These steps should be specific, measurable, and timely, each building upon the last to create momentum and a sense of continuity.

Breaking your goals into micro steps also helps mitigate feelings of intimidation or discouragement that often accompany grand ambitions. A goal seems more achievable and less daunting when dissected into smaller tasks. This helps maintain a positive outlook and ensures that you remain engaged with the task at hand, as each step provides a mini-goal that can be accomplished relatively quickly.

Furthermore, setting goals in this way allows for regular assessment and adjustment. As you progress through your micro steps, you can evaluate what's working and what isn't, making it easier to adapt your approach. This flexibility is crucial in navigating obstacles and refining strategies to better suit your evolving needs or circumstances. It also permits a level of detail and precision in planning that might be overlooked when focusing solely on the end goal.

By embracing setting goals through micro steps, you effectively scaffold your path to success. This method keeps your journey toward achieving big dreams well-organized and less overwhelming and enriches the experience, allowing for growth and learning at every stage. Each small step is a building block, paving the way to the larger triumphs that await, ensuring that every minor achievement is a crucial part of the bigger picture.

The importance of self-assessment and reflection in tracking progress

Self-assessment and reflection are pivotal in any journey of personal or professional development. This practice involves regularly taking stock of your achievements and challenges, providing a comprehensive view of your progress and areas that require more attention or a different approach. It serves as a crucial mechanism for learning and adaptation, enabling you to see what you've accomplished and understand the dynamics of your successes and setbacks.

Self-assessment and reflection allow you to pause and consider the effectiveness of your strategies and actions. By engaging in this introspective process, you can identify patterns in your behavior that either aid or hinder your progress. This insight is invaluable because it equips you with the knowledge to make informed decisions about moving forward more effectively. It's about more than just checking off completed tasks; it involves a deeper analysis of how and why your efforts lead to specific outcomes.

Reflecting on your progress helps cultivate a mindset of continuous improvement. It prompts you to ask critical questions about your methods, timelines, and resources. Are these elements aligned with your goals? Are there adjustments that could lead to better results? This level of questioning fosters a proactive approach to personal growth and problem-solving, encouraging you to always look for ways to enhance efficiency and effectiveness.

Moreover, self-assessment and reflection contribute to emotional and psychological well-being. It allows for celebrating accomplishments and a constructive perspective on less successful endeavors. Recognizing your achievements can be a significant boost to your confidence and motivation. Conversely, understanding your challenges without harsh judgment fosters resilience and a willingness to embrace learning opportunities. It transforms potential discouragement into a motivated reassessment of tactics, thereby maintaining your commitment to your goals.

Incorporating regular self-assessment and reflection into your routine ensures that you remain aligned with your objectives while staying adaptable to change. It enables you to take control of your development process, ensuring that each step you take is purposeful and informed. By making this practice a fundamental part of your strategy, you enhance your ability to achieve your goals and grow and evolve.

Tools and strategies to facilitate micro steps

Tools and strategies to facilitate micro steps are essential in effectively implementing and sustaining a micro steps approach to achieving your goals. These tools and techniques provide the structure and support necessary to make the process manageable, trackable, and adaptable, ensuring that each small step is purposeful and contributes to your overall success.

One effective strategy is to use planning and organization tools, such as planners, apps, or digital calendars, to help you break down your goals into actionable steps and schedule them. These tools allow you to visualize your path forward, allocate time for each task, and set reminders to keep you accountable. By organizing your tasks this way, you can manage your time efficiently and keep your focus on the immediate actions that need your attention.

Another powerful strategy is establishing a routine or system that supports regular action. This might involve daily or weekly habits that incrementally lead to your goal. For instance, if you want to write a book, you might establish a routine of writing a certain number of words or pages daily. By making this a regular part of your day, you lower the psychological barriers to starting, and it becomes part of your natural flow of daily activities.

Progress tracking is also a vital tool in facilitating micro steps. This could be as simple as maintaining a journal where you record completed tasks or using more sophisticated tracking apps that visually represent your progress. Tracking offers the satisfaction of seeing what you have accomplished and helps identify when adjustments may be needed if progress stalls.

Creating support systems can also significantly enhance your ability to stick with micro steps. These might include accountability partners, mentors, or joining groups with similar goals. Such support systems provide external motivation and feedback, which can be crucial when your motivation might wane.

Lastly, it's beneficial to incorporate flexibility into your tools and strategies. Life is dynamic, and your approach to achieving goals should be adaptable. This might mean adjusting your micro-steps as you learn more about what works best for you or as circumstances change. Flexibility ensures that your approach to goal achievement is sustainable over the long term, allowing you to continue progressing even when faced with unexpected challenges.

By employing these tools and strategies, you equip yourself with a robust framework for breaking down big dreams into manageable, achievable micro steps. This simplifies reaching complex goals and enhances your ability to maintain momentum and adapt as needed.

Part II: Applying Micro Steps in Various Aspects of Life

Chapter 4:
Personal Growth and Development

> "Small steps may seem insignificant, but their cumulative effect is profound, turning ordinary routines into extraordinary journeys of growth and fulfillment." - Unknown.

Health and wellness: Incorporating micro-steps into daily routines

Let's delve deeper into each aspect of incorporating micro-steps into your daily routines to enhance your personal growth and development in health and wellness.

Embracing the day with a simple act of hydration can be transformative. By setting a micro goal to drink a glass of water each morning, you're not only replenishing your body's first need after hours of sleep but also setting a tone of self-care that carries through the day. Water is crucial for metabolism, cognitive function, and overall physical health. Encouraging yourself to stay hydrated helps maintain focus, detoxifies the body, and significantly improves skin health and vitality. Over time, this seemingly small habit helps build a foundation for more structured water intake and sets a natural rhythm for healthier living.

Even in minimal amounts, physical activity can disproportionately positively affect your health. Consider incorporating short, manageable bursts of exercise into your daily routine. Three to five minutes of stretching, walking, or simple bodyweight exercises strategically placed throughout the day can alleviate the negative effects of prolonged sitting, boost your metabolism, and improve circulation. These microbursts are manageable, like a full workout might be, and are more likely to become ingrained in your daily life. Gradually, these mini-sessions can cumulatively equate to the benefits of longer exercise routines, enhancing muscular strength and cardiovascular health.

Regarding nutrition, small dietary tweaks can lead to substantial changes. For instance, adding a single serving of vegetables to your dinner plate each night can initiate a gradual shift towards healthier eating habits. This approach introduces more nutrients into your diet and cultivates a palette that appreciates the flavors and textures of whole foods. Over time, you might naturally gravitate towards healthier choices, reducing processed food intake and enjoying the process of meal preparation and mindful eating.

Mental wellness also thrives on small but consistent practices. Allocating just a few minutes of mindfulness or meditation daily can significantly decrease stress and enhance emotional equilibrium. Starting with a brief guided meditation session or a quiet walk after dinner can help clear your mind, reduce anxiety, and bolster your mental resilience. These practices, though small in duration, can profoundly impact your outlook, making you more resilient to stress and more focused on your daily tasks.

Lastly, the power of proper sleep must be balanced in any wellness routine. By shifting your bedtime just 15 minutes earlier, you can gently transition towards better sleep habits without feeling overwhelmed by a drastic change. This minor adjustment can lead to more restful nights, better mood regulation, and enhanced cognitive function, all of which are crucial for maintaining physical and mental health over the long term.

By focusing on these micro steps, you gradually weave a tapestry of habits that promote a healthier, more balanced lifestyle. Each small action is a thread in a larger pattern of personal well-being, proving that sometimes the smallest steps lead to the most significant journeys in pursuing health.

Learning and Skill development: Using micro steps for lifelong learning

As you explore lifelong learning and skill development, micro steps are a powerful strategy for continuous improvement and mastery. Embracing small, incremental steps in your learning journey makes the process more manageable and enriches your engagement with new knowledge and skills over time.

Consider the vast expanse of learning as a series of small, interconnected steps rather than a steep, overwhelming climb. Start by identifying a specific area of interest or a skill you wish to develop. Once pinpointed, break down the learning process into micro-steps that can be easily integrated into your daily routine. For example, if you're interested in learning a new language, dedicate ten minutes each morning to studying basic vocabulary. This practice might seem modest, but over weeks and months, it accumulates into a significant comprehension and communication ability.

The beauty of using micro steps for learning is that it allows for consistent progress without the burnout associated with intense, prolonged study sessions. This approach also aids in retaining information more effectively. The brain benefits from short, frequent learning sessions, a method known as spaced repetition, which has been scientifically shown to improve memory and recall. Revisiting information regularly for brief periods solidifies your understanding and retention of new knowledge.

Additionally, technology can be a valuable ally in implementing micro steps in your learning process. Utilize apps and online platforms designed to facilitate micro-learning. These tools often provide bite-sized lessons that fit perfectly into the small pockets of time throughout your day. Whether listening to a podcast episode during your commute or completing a quick lesson on a mobile learning app while waiting for a meeting, these tools make it easy to turn idle time into productive learning moments.

Another effective strategy is to incorporate micro-steps into existing habits, thus creating a layered learning experience. If you already have a habit of reading before bed, for instance, switch some time to focus on books or articles related to a new skill or knowledge area you're exploring. This method enriches your routine and ensures that your new learning endeavor seamlessly integrates into your life without feeling like an additional burden.

Engage with communities of like-minded learners to deepen your engagement and solidify your learning. Online forums, local workshops, and study groups are excellent for sharing insights and challenges. No matter how brief, each interaction provides new perspectives and deepens your understanding of complex concepts. Moreover, teaching others is a powerful way to enhance your learning. Explain new concepts or skills to a friend or colleague or contribute to discussions. This teaching reinforces your knowledge and uncovers any gaps in your understanding.

Reflection is also crucial to learning through micro steps. Regularly reflecting on what you've learned reinforces the material and allows you to adjust your approach as needed. This could be as simple as spending a few minutes each week reviewing what you've learned, assessing what methods are working, and planning what to focus on in the upcoming days.

Finally, celebrate small victories along the way. Every chapter finished, every new word learned, and every concept mastered, no matter how small, is a step forward in your lifelong learning journey. These celebrations keep motivation high and make the process enjoyable and fulfilling.

By using micro steps for lifelong learning, you are setting yourself up for success in a sustainable way over the long term. This approach makes learning more digestible and more manageable. It ensures that you continuously grow and adapt, keeping your mind and professional skills sharp and relevant in an ever-changing world.

Creativity and hobbies: Cultivating interests through small daily practices

As you nurture your creativity and develop hobbies, adopting micro steps provides a gentle and effective framework for fostering these interests. Cultivating your creative side and engaging in hobbies can often seem daunting, especially when juggling the demands of daily life. However, by integrating small, daily practices into your routine, you can progressively build your skills and enrich your personal and professional life.

Cultivating creativity and hobbies through micro-steps begins with identifying what intrigues you most. Whether painting, writing, gardening, or any other activity that sparks joy and interest, the key is to start with small, manageable commitments that fit easily into your life. For instance, if you are drawn to painting, you might start by sketching for just ten minutes each day. This modest investment of time is enough to slowly develop your skills without requiring a large block of time that might feel overwhelming.

The power of daily practice lies in its ability to transform sporadic interests into enduring passions. Small daily actions help maintain momentum and gradually improve your proficiency. Over time, these minutes add up, significantly advancing your abilities and deepening your engagement with your hobby. Additionally, this approach helps minimize frustration and feeling overwhelmed, which can come with taking on too large a task.

Integrating creativity into your daily life can also be facilitated by strategically using prompts or themes. If writing interests you, choose a daily prompt to write a short paragraph each evening. This structured approach fuels creativity and builds a routine that embeds your hobby into your daily life. Similarly, for those interested in music, learning or practicing a single measure of a song each day can incrementally build up to mastering a whole piece.

Furthermore, leveraging technology can dramatically enhance your daily ability to engage with hobbies. Numerous apps and online communities offer resources, tutorials, and support for any hobby or creative pursuit. Engaging with these platforms can provide structure and inspiration, allowing you to learn from others and share your progress, which can be incredibly motivating.

Community engagement is another enriching aspect of cultivating hobbies and creativity. Joining a local club or online group that shares your interests can provide a sense of accountability, inspiration, and feedback. Interaction with fellow enthusiasts offers social reinforcement and often sparks new ideas, enhancing your creative output. Moreover, community involvement can lead to collaborative projects that may still need to be possible, pushing your creative boundaries and expanding your skill set.

Regular reflection and adaptation are crucial in nurturing your creative interests. Set aside weekly time to reflect on your progress, evaluate what's working, and adjust your practices accordingly. This reflective practice ensures that your activities remain enjoyable and challenging, avoiding stagnation and keeping the excitement alive in your pursuit.

Celebrating small milestones is essential. Whether completing a painting, performing a new song perfectly, or writing a poem that resonates with your feelings, recognizing and celebrating these achievements encourages and sustains your enthusiasm for the hobby.

By embracing micro steps for cultivating creativity and hobbies, you create a sustainable and fulfilling path to developing your interests. This method ensures continuous progress and skill development and seamlessly integrates your passions into your lifestyle, enhancing your personal satisfaction and creative output. This approach proves that with small, consistent steps, you can cultivate a rich, vibrant tapestry of hobbies and creativity that enriches every aspect of your life.

Chapter 5:
Professional and Career Development

"Success is the sum of small efforts, repeated day in and day out."

— Robert Collier

Career progression: Taking micro steps toward career goals

The concept of micro steps truly shines when we think about career progression. It's about breaking down your ultimate career goals into smaller, manageable pieces that feel less daunting and more achievable. This approach isn't just about making incremental progress—it's also about building momentum and creating a sense of continuous achievement.

For instance, if you want to become a department head, identify the skills and experiences required for that position. This could include leadership, communication, and specific industry knowledge. Once you have that list, break it down into micro steps such as taking on a small project to lead at work, enrolling in a part-time leadership course, or setting up regular meetings with a mentor.

Each step might seem small, but collectively, they build your competence and confidence. This method also allows you to adjust your path as you learn more about your strengths, weaknesses, and workplace dynamics. It's about embracing flexibility in your career planning and making adjustments as necessary, which can lead to more personalized and satisfying career development. Moreover, these micro steps can help mitigate the overwhelm that often accompanies the pursuit of big goals, making your professional journey feel more enjoyable and less stressful.

Engaging in this structured yet adaptable progression can create a powerful growth narrative in your career, where each small success fuels the next, leading to meaningful change over time.

Productivity and efficiency: Small changes for a more productive workflow

When we turn our attention to productivity and efficiency, the principle of small changes can make a significant difference in refining our workflow. This approach identifies little tweaks and adjustments that can be made daily or weekly, leading to a smoother and more efficient work process.

For example, consider the arrangement of your workspace. A minor adjustment, such as organizing your desk or optimizing the placement of frequently used tools and documents, can save you a surprising amount of time each day. Similarly, adopting a new digital tool for task management might seem like a small step, but it can profoundly impact how effectively you prioritize and track your daily activities.

Another micro-step is restructuring how you handle email. Instead of constantly checking and responding to emails throughout the day, you might set specific times for this task to minimize distractions and improve focus on more critical tasks.

Additionally, introducing short, regular breaks throughout your workday can prevent burnout and improve mental clarity and energy levels, making you more productive.

Each of these small changes may seem inconsequential when viewed in isolation, but when implemented together, they can streamline your workflow, reduce wasted time, and enhance your overall productivity. This iterative process of making small adjustments allows you to continuously refine your working habits and environment, adapting to changes and challenges with greater agility.

Leadership and interpersonal skills: Incremental improvements in communication and leadership

Let's explore how incremental improvements can enhance leadership and interpersonal skills. This aspect of professional development is crucial because effective communication and leadership are about having authority and how you connect with and inspire others.

Consider the skill of active listening, a fundamental component of effective communication and leadership. Improving in this area can be as simple as practicing mindful listening in your daily interactions—paying close attention to what others are saying without planning your response while they speak. This small change can dramatically improve the quality of your interactions and the trust you build with colleagues.

Another micro step could be regularly seeking feedback on your communication style and leadership techniques. This could involve asking for constructive criticism from peers and mentors and then making small adjustments based on that feedback, such as working on your tone, body language, or the clarity of your instructions.

Improving your storytelling skills is another incremental step that can significantly impact you. Leaders must often motivate and inspire, and being able to craft and convey compelling narratives about your team's goals and successes can engage and energize your audience. This might start with something as simple as sharing a small personal success story at a team meeting to illustrate a point more vividly.

Additionally, enhancing your conflict resolution skills by adopting techniques such as empathetic negotiation and clear, respectful communication can prevent misunderstandings and build a more collaborative team environment. This could begin with learning about conflict resolution strategies and then practicing them in low-stakes situations to build confidence.

Each of these incremental improvements helps you build a repertoire of leadership and interpersonal skills that can significantly enhance your leadership effectiveness and how others perceive your leadership. Over time, these small steps can transform your ability to lead with empathy, clarity, and inspiration, fundamentally changing your professional interactions and leadership style.

Chapter 6:
Financial Well-being

"The journey of a thousand miles begins with one step." — Lao Tzu.

Budgeting and saving: Small financial habits for long-term security

When we explore the theme of financial well-being, we focus particularly on the importance of budgeting and saving. These small, manageable financial habits lay a solid foundation for long-term security. Let's delve deeper into how these seemingly minor steps can significantly impact your financial future.

Budgeting is not just about restraining spending; it's about understanding and controlling where your money goes so you can make decisions that align with your long-term goals. By setting up a budget, you categorize your expenses, which range from necessities like rent and groceries to discretionary spending on entertainment and hobbies. This process should provide a clear picture of your financial landscape, allowing you to identify areas where you can cut back without feeling deprived, thus enabling your savings to grow.

On the other hand, saving is about looking forward and preparing for both the expected and unexpected. The act of saving is empowering because it builds a buffer against life's uncertainties and paves the way for future investments or guilt-free splurges. The key to successful saving is consistency; even small amounts set aside regularly can compound over time to create a substantial nest egg. Consider saving as paying your future self, ensuring you have the resources you need for emergencies, retirement, or fulfilling your dreams.

Budgeting and saving form a synergistic duo, each practice informing and enhancing the other. A robust budget provides a roadmap for your spending, making it easier to find opportunities to save. Conversely, regular saving habits can influence your budgeting strategies, as the satisfaction of growing savings can motivate further efficiency in spending.

Embracing these practices as part of your routine requires minimal daily effort but promises substantial rewards. As you incorporate these small financial habits, you'll notice a growing sense of control and confidence in your financial situation. This empowerment is the essence of economic well-being, achieved through continuous, incremental improvement. So, take those small steps today to secure a stable and prosperous tomorrow.

Investing: Starting small with investments for future growth

Let's focus on investing, a fundamental element of financial well-being that centers on starting small for substantial future growth. Investing might seem daunting at first, especially if you're new to it, but beginning with small steps can lead to significant benefits down the line.

Investing is about putting your money to work so it can grow over time. Starting small means you don't have to wait until you have a large sum. Instead, you can begin with whatever amount you are comfortable with, which helps mitigate risk and eases you into the world of investments. This could be as simple as investing in a mutual fund or a retirement plan allowing automatic deductions from your paycheck. The idea is to make investing a habit that becomes a regular part of your financial strategy without feeling overwhelming.

The beauty of starting small is that it leverages the power of compound interest. Over time, even small investments grow as the returns generate further returns. This compounding effect can turn modest, regular contributions into a considerable sum over decades, essentially earning money on your initial investment and the accumulated gains from preceding periods.

Moreover, beginning with smaller investments allows you to learn as you go, gaining confidence and understanding of various investment vehicles and market conditions without the pressure of having too much at stake. It's an educational journey as much as a financial one, which prepares you to make more informed decisions and potentially larger investments in the future.

By integrating investing into your financial habits, you ensure that your money isn't just sitting idle but is actively contributing to your future financial stability and goals. This approach not only cultivates a healthy financial mindset but also sets a foundation for increasing wealth and security as you become more adept at managing and expanding your investment portfolio.

So, start small, but start now. Consistent, thoughtful investments can make all the difference, allowing you to grow your wealth gradually and securely.

Debt reduction: Micro step strategies to reduce financial burden

Now, let's explore the vital area of debt reduction, which focuses on employing a micro-step strategy to lessen your financial burden. Reducing debt is essential to achieving financial well-being and can be approached with manageable, incremental steps that make the task less intimidating and more achievable.

Debt can often feel overwhelming, but breaking down your approach into smaller, more manageable steps can transform the process into a more positive experience. One effective micro-step strategy is to prioritize your debts—start by identifying which ones carry the highest interest rates and target those first. This method, often referred to as the avalanche method, ensures that you reduce the interest you pay over time, which can significantly decrease the total amount you end up paying.

Another useful micro-step is to set up automated payments for your minimum dues to ensure you never miss a payment. This can help improve your credit score and avoid additional fees. Once the minimum payments are under control, additional funds can be directed toward paying down the principal of the highest-interest debts, accelerating the debt reduction process.

Additionally, revising your budget regularly to find extra savings that can be redirected toward your debt can be very effective. Even small amounts, when consistently applied to your debt, can lead to significant reductions over time. This could mean cutting back on non-essential expenses or finding small ways to increase your income, such as doing freelance work or selling items you no longer need.

By focusing on these micro steps, you can gradually reduce your debt load without feeling too drastic or restricted. These steps help decrease your debt and build healthy financial habits to prevent future debt accumulation. Remember, the key is consistency and persistence; small but steady efforts will lead to big changes in your financial health and reduce the overall stress associated with debt.

There are a few more nuances to consider when discussing the power of tiny financial steps that can be tremendously beneficial.

Emergency Savings: Establishing an emergency fund is an often overlooked but critical aspect of financial stability. Starting small by setting aside even a tiny portion of your income regularly can build a cushion that protects you against unexpected expenses, such as medical emergencies, urgent home repairs, or sudden job loss. The goal is typically to have enough saved to cover three to six months of living expenses, but even starting with a goal of $500 or $1000 can be a significant step towards financial resilience.

Spending Awareness: Cultivating a deep awareness of your spending habits can also serve as a micro-step toward better financial health. Simply tracking all your monthly expenses, whether through a budgeting app, spreadsheet, or pen and paper—can give you valuable insights into where your money goes. This awareness alone can often prompt adjustments in spending behavior, leading to increased savings without feeling constrained.

Financial Education: Investing in your financial education is another small step with potentially large dividends. Learning about basic economic concepts like interest rates, the stock market, insurance, and retirement planning can demystify many aspects of money management. This knowledge empowers you to make informed decisions and increases your confidence in handling more complex financial matters as they arise.

Using Technology: Leveraging technology can simplify the execution of these small financial steps. Numerous apps and tools can help automate savings, track spending, and even regularly invest small amounts of money. Technology can remove some of the burdens of managing finances and help you maintain consistency in your efforts.

Mindset Shifts: Adopting a mindset that values small gains can profoundly impact your financial health. Celebrating each small victory—whether paying off a small debt, saving an extra $50, or sticking to your monthly budget—reinforces positive financial behaviors and motivates you to continue progressing.

By focusing on these additional aspects and incorporating them into your daily routine, you can enhance the impact of your tiny steps toward financial security. It's all about building momentum with manageable actions that collectively lead to substantial improvements in your financial life.

Part III: Overcoming Obstacles with Micro Steps

Chapter 7:
Facing Challenges Head-on

"The greater the obstacle, the more glory in overcoming it."

—Molière

Identifying and addressing common setbacks in the journey of continuous improvement

In your journey toward continuous improvement, it's vital to recognize and confront the common setbacks you may encounter. Understanding these challenges is the first step towards turning them into opportunities for growth and learning.

One of the most frequent hurdles is feeling overwhelmed by the scale of your goals. When ambitions seem too lofty, achieving them can appear daunting. Break down these larger goals into smaller, manageable tasks. This makes the process less intimidating and provides frequent moments of achievement that can boost your morale and motivation.

Resistance to change is another significant barrier. It's a natural human tendency to prefer the comfort of familiar routines and practices, even when they are less effective. To overcome this, emphasize the benefits of the new methods and involve yourself deeply in the learning process. Engage with the changes actively and allow yourself to experience the improvements they bring firsthand, making the transition more meaningful and less resistant.

Procrastination often creeps in, particularly when tasks seem difficult or unpleasant. This can derail your progress and diminish your enthusiasm. Combat this by setting clear, immediate deadlines and creating a rewarding environment celebrating small victories. This approach helps maintain momentum and reinforces the habit of taking consistent action, regardless of the task's nature.

Lastly, a lack of immediate results can lead to discouragement. Continuous improvement is typically a slow and incremental process. Setting realistic expectations and appreciating the value of small gains is crucial. Regularly reflect on how these small steps contribute to your larger goals and remind yourself that perseverance is key in this journey.

By identifying these setbacks and adopting strategies to address them, you equip yourself with the tools needed to face challenges head-on and continue on your path of continuous improvement with resilience and determination.

Strategies for maintaining motivation and focus when progress seems slow

Maintaining motivation and focus can be particularly challenging when progress seems slow, a common scenario in pursuing continuous improvement. Here are several strategies to help keep your spirits high and your eyes on the prize, even when advancements are minimal.

Firstly, keep a visual representation of your progress. This could be a chart, a journal, or a simple checklist you update regularly. Visual aids are a concrete reminder of how far you've come, even when each step forward is small. They provide a sense of accomplishment and a visual affirmation that your efforts add up.

Secondly, reconnect with the reasons why you started this journey. Regularly reflecting on your initial motivations can reignite your passion and reframe your perspective on the current pace of progress. Whether it's personal development, professional advancement, or another goal, reminding yourself of the fundamental reasons for your efforts can be a powerful motivator.

In addition, set up regular rewards for yourself. Establish small rewards for completing tasks or milestones, regardless of how minor they may seem. This could be as simple as treating yourself to a favorite coffee, enjoying a movie night, or taking a day off. Rewards help make the journey enjoyable and associate positive feelings with completing even the smallest tasks.

It's also beneficial to share your goals and progress with someone you trust. A friend, colleague, or mentor who understands your objectives and can encourage you can make a significant difference. They can offer support during slower periods, provide accountability, and celebrate your small wins with you, which can greatly enhance your motivation.

Lastly, adjust your goals as needed. Sometimes, slow progress is a sign that your approach might need tweaking. Don't hesitate to reassess and modify your goals to make them more achievable. This isn't a step back but rather a strategic adjustment that can lead to more consistent and sustainable progress.

Implementing these strategies can help you maintain a high level of motivation and focus, even when the pace of improvement is slower than expected. These techniques support your immediate goals and enhance your resilience and commitment to continuous growth.

We've touched on some essential strategies for staying motivated and focused. To expand on these, incorporating a structured routine and using positive affirmations might also be beneficial.

Building a Daily Routine: A consistent daily routine can significantly improve focus and productivity. Setting times for concentrated work, reflection, and breaks can reduce decision fatigue and ensure that you steadily progress toward your goals, even on less motivated days. Customize your routine to balance intense work periods with sufficient downtime to avoid burnout.

Employing Positive Affirmations: Positive affirmations are a powerful tool for maintaining a positive mindset and combating discouragement. Regularly affirming your skills and dedication creates a positive mental space that supports ongoing perseverance and resilience. Begin your day or approach challenging tasks by reaffirming your capabilities and commitment to achieving your objectives.

Chapter 8:
Adapting and Adjusting Strategies

"It is not the strongest of the species that survives, nor the most intelligent; it is the most adaptable to change." — Charles Darwin.

The importance of flexibility and adaptability in pursuing long-term goals

Flexibility and adaptability are crucial traits to cultivate when pursuing long-term goals. They allow you to navigate the inevitable changes and challenges, ensuring your path to success is resilient and responsive.

The journey toward any significant achievement is rarely linear. It involves unexpected obstacles, shifts in circumstances, and evolving personal or professional landscapes. Flexibility means you're prepared to reassess and modify your strategies as needed. This could involve altering your timelines, redefining your goals, or adopting new methods if the current ones are no longer effective.

Adaptability goes beyond minor adjustments; it involves a deeper willingness to transform your approach based on new information or feedback. It's about being open to learning and growth, even if it means stepping out of your comfort zone. This trait is particularly valuable in today's fast-paced world, where new technologies, tools, and ways of thinking can rapidly make old methods obsolete.

By nurturing a mindset that welcomes change, you equip yourself to tackle challenges more creatively and seize opportunities that rigid adherence to a plan might miss. This keeps your journey towards long-term goals dynamic and enhances your personal and professional growth.

In essence, flexibility and adaptability must be considered. They are the keys to surviving and thriving in pursuing your long-term ambitions, allowing you to adjust your sails when the wind changes direction and continue moving forward effectively.

Knowing when and how to adjust your micro steps for maximum impact

Knowing when and how to adapt your micro steps is essential for maximizing their impact in pursuing long-term goals. These adjustments ensure that your actions align with your evolving objectives and circumstances, enhancing your efforts, efficiency, and effectiveness.

Regularly reviewing and evaluating your progress is the first step in making these adjustments. This doesn't just mean checking if tasks are completed but also assessing whether these tasks are still most effectively driving you toward your goals. Set periodic reviews—weekly, monthly, or quarterly—to reflect on what's working and what isn't. This will help you identify the need for adjustments early, preventing wasted effort on outdated strategies.

Understanding how to adjust involves considering both the scale and the direction of your micro steps. For example, if a particular approach yields better results than expected, you might amplify your efforts in that area or speed up your timeline. Conversely, if progress is slower than anticipated, simplifying tasks or extending deadlines might be necessary to accommodate more realistic expectations.

Additionally, stay informed about new tools, methods, or information that could enhance your approach. Embracing innovation can lead to more effective strategies and be critical in adjusting your steps toward maximum impact.

Finally, be prepared to pivot completely if certain strategies consistently fail to produce results. Sometimes, the best adjustment is a substantial change in approach, which can open up new pathways to success that were previously unconsidered.

By effectively adjusting your micro steps, you ensure that your approach to achieving long-term goals is as dynamic and responsive as your challenges. This adaptability increases your chances of success and keeps you engaged and motivated throughout your journey.

Discussing the importance of feedback and collaboration in refining your approach might further enrich this chapter on adapting and adjusting strategies.

Incorporating Feedback: Regularly soliciting and integrating feedback is crucial for continual improvement and adaptability. Feedback can come from various sources, such as mentors, peers, or customer responses. It provides you with external perspectives that can highlight blind spots in your strategies and suggest new ideas for enhancement. Embrace positive and constructive feedback as tools for learning and refining your approach to achieving your goals.

Fostering Collaboration: Collaboration can also significantly enhance the adaptability of your strategies. Working with others brings diverse skills and viewpoints, offering new insights and approaches. Collaborative environments can foster innovation and provide support, making it easier to adjust strategies as challenges arise. Consider forming partnerships or joining networks that align with your goals to maximize the benefits of collective intelligence.

Focusing on feedback and collaboration enriches your understanding and approach and builds a support network to propel you toward your long-term goals more effectively. These elements can be pivotal in maintaining a flexible and adaptive strategy, ensuring you are well-prepared to navigate the complexities of any long-term endeavor.

Part IV: Sustaining and Scaling Up

Chapter 9:

Maintaining Momentum

"Success is the sum of small efforts, repeated day in and day out." — Robert Collier.

Keeping the flame of motivation burning with ongoing micro steps

To maintain momentum in any journey of continuous improvement, it is crucial to keep the flame of motivation burning by incorporating micro-steps into daily routines. These small, manageable actions help sustain progress and prevent burnout. By setting mini-goals that are achievable and aligned with larger objectives, individuals can experience frequent successes, which boost their morale and encourage persistence. This process of breaking down tasks also allows for immediate feedback and adjustments, ensuring that efforts remain effective and relevant. Furthermore, celebrating these small victories can reinforce the importance of each step towards the overarching goal. It's essential to remember that consistency in these micro steps cultivates habits that become second nature, thus perpetuating a cycle of positive behavior and continuous improvement. This approach makes the journey more manageable and keeps the excitement and engagement levels high, as there is always something new to achieve just around the corner.

As individuals continue to incorporate micro-steps into their routines, it's beneficial to periodically reassess and recalibrate their goals. This ongoing evaluation helps to ensure that the steps remain relevant and appropriately challenging, preventing stagnation and maintaining interest. Additionally, connecting with a community or support group that shares similar improvement goals can provide a valuable source of motivation. Such communities offer encouragement, share tips, and celebrate milestones together, which can significantly enhance one's commitment and enthusiasm.

Leveraging technology can also play a pivotal role in maintaining momentum. Tools and apps designed for tracking progress, scheduling tasks, and providing reminders can simplify the management of micro steps. This technological support makes it easier to stay on track and visualize progress, which can be incredibly motivating. By integrating these strategies, the path toward continuous improvement becomes clear, structured, dynamic, and adaptable, ensuring sustained motivation and effectiveness over time.

Another aspect of maintaining momentum with micro steps is incorporating reflection and learning from each journey phase. Taking time to reflect on what has worked and hasn't allows for a deeper understanding of one's methods and outcomes. This introspection can fuel further motivation, as it highlights areas for improvement and potential adjustments in tactics. Learning from successes and setbacks is crucial, as it encourages a growth mindset and fosters resilience, making overcoming challenges in future endeavors easier.

Additionally, it's important to keep the process enjoyable and varied. Introducing new micro steps or varying existing ones can prevent monotony and renew interest. This might involve changing the context or scope of tasks, experimenting with different time frames, or integrating new tools or methods. Keeping the process fresh ensures that motivation remains high and that the journey towards improvement continues to be engaging and rewarding. By staying flexible and open to change, one can effectively sustain momentum and keep the flame of motivation burning brightly.

Building a supportive community for encouragement and accountability

Building a supportive community for encouragement and accountability is vital for sustaining momentum in any long-term improvement process. This community can comprise peers, mentors, family members, or even online groups with similar goals or challenges. The presence of a supportive network creates a sense of belonging and significantly boosts motivation through encouragement and recognition of one's efforts.

A community fosters a collaborative environment where members exchange ideas, strategies, and experiences. This exchange enriches each member's journey, providing fresh perspectives and innovative approaches to overcoming obstacles. Additionally, the community serves as a source of accountability. Knowing that others know one's goals and progress can spur individuals to remain committed, even when facing difficulties or motivation wanes.

Moreover, a supportive community can offer emotional support, which is crucial during setbacks or when goals seem distant. The empathy and understanding from others on similar paths can alleviate the sense of isolation that sometimes accompanies personal and professional challenges. This emotional backing helps maintain a positive outlook and resilience, essential for continuous improvement.

Finally, the community can evolve into a platform for celebrating big and small successes. These celebrations reinforce the value of every member's effort and achievement, enhancing the collective enthusiasm and commitment to shared goals. This sense of collective achievement and progress keeps everyone motivated and focused on the path ahead.

Conditions and circumstances can change in any long-term improvement process, impacting the relevance and effectiveness of predetermined plans and micro steps. Emphasizing the importance of adaptability allows individuals to adjust their strategies in response to such changes, ensuring that their efforts remain aligned with their goals.

Incorporating adaptability involves encouraging individuals to remain open to new information and experiences, which can provide unexpected opportunities for growth and improvement. Promoting a mindset that views challenges and changes not as obstacles but as catalysts for innovation and creativity is also helpful. This perspective can transform potentially demotivating situations into exciting new avenues for development.

Additionally, practical tips on cultivating adaptability—such as setting aside regular times for reflection and review, practicing proactive problem-solving, and seeking diverse perspectives within the community—can provide readers with actionable steps to enhance their resilience and flexibility.

Finally, discussing the psychological benefits of adaptability, such as increased confidence, reduced stress, and greater overall satisfaction, could highlight the holistic benefits of embracing change as part of the continuous improvement journey. These elements can help maintain momentum by ensuring the process is dynamic and responsive to the evolving personal and professional landscapes.

Chapter 10
From Micro Steps to Macro Leaps

"Growth is never by chance; it results from forces working together."

— James Cash Penney

Recognizing when small steps lead to big jumps in progress

In the journey of personal and professional development, the significance of small, deliberate steps must be addressed. These simple and seemingly insignificant micro steps can lead to significant breakthroughs, propelling individuals from incremental progress to substantial leaps in their goals and achievements. This transformative process begins with recognizing these critical junctures, where small actions translate into larger results.

One key aspect of recognizing when small steps are about to lead to big jumps is the accumulation of small wins. Over time, these accumulate, creating a solid foundation of skills, knowledge, and confidence. This foundation is crucial because it prepares one for more complex challenges and opportunities. As these skills and competencies build up, individuals are at a tipping point where the next small step can unexpectedly catalyze a major advance.

Monitoring progress plays a pivotal role in this process. Tracking small achievements helps identify patterns and trends when a series of actions coalesce into a significant change. This monitoring can be as simple as maintaining a daily journal or as complex as using digital tools to track and analyze data. The insight gained from this monitoring enables one to adjust strategies, capitalize on momentum, and push through plateaus that might otherwise go unnoticed.

Feedback is another critical element in this journey. Whether it comes from self-reflection, peers, mentors, or performance metrics, feedback provides invaluable insights into what works and does not. It often highlights whether the small steps lead towards the intended goal or if a course correction is necessary. This feedback loop ensures that the steps are small and right.

Finally, it is essential to cultivate a mindset that values and recognizes the power of small steps. This involves embracing patience and persistence and understanding that significant achievements are often the result of many small, consistent efforts. This mindset shift is fundamental in transforming how one approaches goals, making it easier to recognize when these efforts are on the brink of yielding significant results.

By understanding and acknowledging these elements, individuals can better recognize when their series of micro steps are poised to make a macro leap, allowing them to strategically leverage these moments for maximum impact. This recognition boosts motivation and reinforces the belief in continuous improvement through small, manageable increments.

Leveraging the power of micro steps to achieve ambitious goals

Leveraging the power of micro steps to achieve ambitious goals is a strategy that harnesses the seemingly modest but cumulative effects of small actions. This approach breaks down large, daunting objectives into manageable, actionable increments, making the process less overwhelming and more achievable. By focusing on these smaller, doable tasks, individuals can maintain steady progress and motivation, even amid ambitious and long-term goals.

"Tiny Triumphs: The Power of Micro Steps in Achieving Continuous Improvement"

The initial step in this strategy involves setting clear, well-defined goals and then deconstructing these into smaller, specific tasks. This decomposition clarifies what needs to be done and makes organizing efforts and prioritizing tasks easier. Each small step is designed to be a building block that moves an individual closer to the larger objective. For example, if the goal is to write a book, breaking it down into daily writing sessions of a few hundred words can transform what seems like an enormous project into daily tasks that are simple and feasible.

As these tasks are completed, they provide a sense of accomplishment and momentum. This psychological boost is crucial as it sustains motivation over time. Regularly completing small tasks reinforces the belief that the goal is attainable, and each small victory builds confidence. Moreover, this segmented approach allows for continuous assessment and adjustment. As each micro-step is completed, one can evaluate the effectiveness of their strategy and make necessary adjustments without being overwhelmed by the scale of the overall goal.

Another aspect of leveraging micro steps is reducing procrastination and enhancing focus. Large goals can often seem intimidating and can lead to avoidance behaviors. By concentrating on small, immediate tasks, individuals can avoid the paralysis that comes with larger challenges. Each task becomes a mini-goal, providing a clear focus for daily activities and reducing the mental burden associated with bigger objectives.

Incorporating regular feedback loops into this process is also vital. Whether through self-assessment or input from others, feedback helps refine the approach and ensure that each step effectively contributes to the ultimate goal. This responsiveness to feedback ensures that the path to the goal remains flexible and adaptable to changing circumstances or insights gained along the way.

Finally, celebrating the completion of micro steps can reinforce their value and keep the momentum alive. Acknowledging these small successes boosts morale and embeds a habit of persistence and dedication toward achieving larger ambitions.

In essence, leveraging the power of micro steps transforms the journey toward ambitious goals from a daunting endeavor into a series of achievable, confidence-building tasks. This strategy makes large goals more attainable and enriches the journey with regular achievements and continuous learning.

Planning for long-term growth and continuous improvement

Planning for long-term growth and continuous improvement is a strategic process that ensures sustained progress and development over time. This approach involves setting a clear vision for the future, establishing long-term goals, and implementing a continuous evaluation and adaptation system. Focusing on immediate and future needs helps individuals and organizations achieve their current objectives and evolve and thrive over time.

The foundation of planning for long-term growth lies in setting a clear and compelling vision that outlines where one wants to be in the future. This vision serves as a guiding star, helping to align short-term actions with long-term objectives. This vision must be inspirational and realistic, providing a sense of direction and being attainable.

Once the vision is set, the next step is to establish long-term goals that are specific, measurable, achievable, relevant, and time-bound (SMART). These goals act as benchmarks for progress and help structure the journey towards the vision. Breaking these long-term goals into smaller, intermediate objectives makes the process manageable and ensures that each step is directed towards eventual larger successes.

Creating a culture of regular reflection and learning is essential to plan for continuous improvement. This involves setting up mechanisms for feedback and review, such as periodic performance evaluations against set goals. These reviews should assess what has been achieved and identify areas for improvement and potential adjustments in strategy. Continuous learning from successes and failures is crucial as it fosters adaptability—an essential attribute in today's ever-changing environment.

Another key component is integrating flexibility within the plan. While having a structured plan is important, remaining open to changes and new opportunities is equally crucial. Adapting and modifying goals in response to new information, changing conditions, or unexpected challenges is vital for long-term sustainability and growth.

Incorporating technology and innovative practices can also enhance the ability to plan effectively for long-term growth. Leveraging tools for data analysis, project management, and performance tracking can provide deeper insights, improve efficiency, and facilitate better decision-making. These tools help accurately measure progress and identify trends that need to be visible through casual observation.

Finally, it is important to embed the principles of resilience and persistence within the planning process. Long-term planning is not just about setting a course; it's also about being prepared to endure challenges and setbacks without losing sight of the ultimate goals. Building resilience involves developing emotional and strategic capacities to handle the highs and lows during the journey.

Planning for long-term growth and continuous improvement is an iterative and strategic process that focuses on achieving set goals and fostering an environment of learning and adaptability.

Doing so ensures that growth is not a temporary spike in progress but a sustainable and evolving path forward.

Case Studies and Examples: A prime example of effective long-term planning can be seen in the transformation of XYZ Corp, a small software company that, over five years, grew into a tech giant. Key to their success was the incremental refinement of their product and processes, punctuated by regular strategic reviews. Each review allowed them to adapt to the shifting tech landscape, demonstrating the power of flexibility combined with consistent effort. Another inspiring story comes from a non-profit organization that significantly impacted regional development by implementing small-scale community engagement projects and gradually expanding them. These examples illustrate that continuous small improvements can lead to substantial business or community work achievements.

Tools and Resources: Various tools can be instrumental in replicating such success. Asana and Trello are excellent for project management, helping track tasks and deadlines effectively. For habit formation and daily goal tracking, apps like Habitica gamify the process, making it engaging and motivational. "The Lean Startup" by Eric Ries also provides invaluable insights into applying continuous innovation to drive a startup's growth.

Expert Insights: Expert opinions are invaluable. For instance, Dr. Jane Smith, a renowned business strategist, suggests, "The key to sustained success is regular strategic reflection. It allows organizations to pivot quickly and effectively in response to external changes." Such insights underline the importance of adaptability and proactive planning in long-term growth.

Interactive Elements: To engage with these ideas actively, readers might reflect on the following questions:

What small steps can you start with today that will contribute to your long-term vision?

How can you incorporate regular reviews into your personal or professional life to ensure continuous improvement?

Implementing these reflections could involve setting monthly personal reviews or establishing a feedback mechanism within one's work team.

Common Pitfalls and How to Avoid Them: Common obstacles include loss of motivation and resource misallocation. To combat these, setting up a system of small rewards for each completed task can maintain motivation. Regularly assessing resource allocation and adjusting plans ensures that efforts are well-spent and goals remain achievable.

Sustainability Considerations: Finally, sustainability is crucial. This encompasses environmental sustainability and ensuring that pursuing business goals does not detriment personal well-being. Strategies include implementing policies encouraging work-life balance and making business decisions considering long-term ecological impacts.

Conclusion

Reflecting on the Journey: The Transformative Power of Micro Steps in Personal and Professional Life

As we conclude our exploration of the power of micro steps in achieving continuous improvement, it's important to reflect on the transformative journey that has unfolded through the pages of this book. We have witnessed how tiny, deliberate actions, consistently applied, can lead to significant changes in a wide array of areas—from personal well-being to organizational success.

Personal Transformation

In personal development, the micro-steps approach has proven especially powerful. Consider the story of Emily, who tackled her anxiety by implementing small daily practices of mindfulness and journaling. Over time, these practices didn't just help manage her anxiety; they transformed her entire approach to life, fostering a sense of peace and resilience that permeated all her relationships and endeavors.

Similarly, John's journey to physical health through incremental changes in diet and exercise highlights how small, sustainable shifts can lead to lasting habits. Instead of overwhelming himself with a complete lifestyle overhaul, John introduced one healthy habit at a time, eventually leading to a loss of 30 pounds over a year and significantly improving his cardiovascular health.

Professional Advancement

The micro-steps philosophy has facilitated profound organizational changes on the professional front. Take the example of a small tech startup that improved employee engagement by introducing weekly feedback sessions. Initially, these sessions were brief and focused on minor improvements. However, they became a cornerstone of the company's culture, leading to increased innovation, employee satisfaction, and retention rates.

Another case is a manufacturing plant that reduced waste and increased efficiency by implementing small, daily checks and balances. By empowering every employee to suggest micro improvements, the plant improved its operational efficiency and fostered a culture of ownership and accountability among its workforce.

Psychological Benefits

Beyond the tangible outcomes, the psychological benefits of the micro-steps approach are equally compelling. Breaking down daunting goals into manageable chunks makes the process less intimidating and more achievable, significantly boosting motivation and commitment. This approach reduces the fear of failure, as setbacks are minor and manageable, not catastrophic.

Cultural Shift

Finally, embracing micro steps can lead to a cultural shift in how success is perceived. It encourages a mindset that values consistent effort and gradual progress over sporadic leaps. It teaches us that patience and persistence can lead to remarkable personal and professional achievements.

Looking Forward

As you reflect on these stories and the principles discussed, consider how the micro-steps approach can be applied continuously in your own life. Whether your goals are improving health, learning new skills, enhancing relationships, or driving professional growth, remember that sustainable change often comes not from grand gestures but small, consistent actions.

This book reminds us that every step counts and that each small action is a building block for a better future. Embrace the journey of micro steps and let them guide you to a life of continuous improvement and lasting fulfillment.

A Call to Action: Start Your Micro Step Journey Towards Continuous Improvement

As this book comes to a close, it's not merely an end but a potential beginning of your transformative journey through micro steps. This isn't just a recommendation—it's an invitation to embark on a path of continuous improvement that could redefine your life. Let's turn these insights into action and see how even the smallest steps can lead to monumental gains.

Identify Your Starting Point

Reflect on areas in your life or work where improvement could bring significant value. Please choose a location that deeply matters to you, whether it's your health, relationships, professional skills, or mental well-being. This connection will fuel your motivation to persist even when the journey gets challenging.

Set Small, Achievable Goals

With your focus area in mind, define small, achievable goals. For example, consider integrating brief physical activity sessions into your daily routine to improve your health or choose healthier food choices one meal at a time. If professional development is your target, spend a few minutes each day reading industry articles or practicing a new skill relevant to your job.

Embrace Consistency and Patience

Adopt a mindset that values consistency over intensity and patience over immediacy. The journey of micro steps is not about sprinting to the finish line; it's about moving steadily towards it.

Understand that real change is often invisible in its early stages, and visible results will follow your persistent efforts over time.

Track and Reflect

Keeping a log of your progress is crucial. It lets you see how far you've come and adjust your strategies. Whether through a journal, an app, or a simple checklist, find a tracking method that works for you. Regular reflection will help you stay aligned with your goals and remember why you started.

Celebrate Every Small Victory

Recognition of small successes plays a critical role in sustaining motivation. Whether you stick to your plan for a week, learn a new word in a foreign language, or manage to meditate for five minutes every day, celebrate these achievements. These celebrations reinforce your resolve and remind you that progress is still progress, regardless of size.

Spread the Word

As you experience the benefits of micro steps, encourage others by sharing your journey. Whether through social media, blogs, or casual conversations, discussing your progress can inspire others to embark on their journeys. This strengthens your commitment and builds a supportive community around gradual improvement and resilience.

Your Journey Begins Now

There is no perfect time to start other than now. Embrace the micro steps approach and let each small action propel you towards a better future. This book is your foundation; your actions are the bricks that will build your improved self. Remember, every effort counts in pursuing continuous improvement, no matter how small.

Anticipate Challenges and Strategize Overcoming Them

As you embark on your journey of micro steps, it's important to recognize that challenges and setbacks are inevitable. Anticipating these obstacles is not a sign of pessimism but a strategy for resilience. Here are some common challenges you might face and ways to navigate them:

Loss of Motivation: It's normal for enthusiasm to wane over time. To combat this, remind yourself of the reasons you started this journey. Revisiting your goals and the benefits you've already observed can reignite your motivation. Also, try mixing up your activities to keep your routine fresh and engaging.

Time Management Issues: Finding time for new habits can be difficult, especially with a busy schedule. Consider integrating micro-steps into existing routines. For example, if you want to read more, you could do so during your morning commute or while waiting for appointments.

Feeling Overwhelmed: If you ever feel overwhelmed by your goals, it might indicate that your steps need to be bigger. Break them down further into even smaller, more manageable tasks. Remember, the essence of micro steps is that they are supposed to be small and easy to manage.

Dealing with Failure: Only some days will go as planned. When you face setbacks, treat them as learning opportunities rather than failures. Analyze what went wrong and how you can adjust your approach. This reflective practice builds resilience and flexibility.

Seeking Support: Sometimes, we need a little extra help. Don't hesitate to seek support from friends, family, or even professionals like coaches or mentors. Sharing your challenges and seeking advice can provide new perspectives and solutions.

By anticipating these challenges and equipping yourself with strategies to overcome them, you're more likely to maintain your momentum and stay committed to your journey of continuous improvement. Every challenge overcome is not just a step in the right direction—it's also a testament to your growth and resilience.

Appendices

Appendix A: Additional Resources for Further Exploration

To continue your journey toward mastering micro steps and embracing continuous improvement, we've created a list of resources that offer valuable insights and practical advice. These resources are designed to complement the lessons from this book and help you expand your understanding and application of these powerful principles.

Books

1. **"Atomic Habits" by James Clear** - This book offers a comprehensive guide to building good habits, breaking bad ones, and mastering the tiny behaviors that lead to remarkable results.
2. **"The Slight Edge" by Jeff Olson** - Olson explains how making small daily improvements can lead to success and why those small, seemingly insignificant steps contribute to profound happiness.
3. **"The Compound Effect" by Darren Hardy** - Hardy illustrates how small, incremental changes can create a massive impact over time, aligning well with the philosophy of micro steps.

Websites

1. **Lifehacker**—This blog offers tips, tricks, and downloads for getting things done more efficiently and effectively.
2. **Tiny Buddha** is a site focused on simple wisdom for complex lives. It offers articles on personal development, mental health, and minimalism.

3. **Zen Habits**—Created by Leo Babauta, this blog is about finding simplicity and mindfulness in daily life and focusing on habits that can transform one's life.

Articles

1. **"The Power of Small Wins" by Teresa Amabile and Steven Kramer** (Harvard Business Review) - This article explores how incremental progress in meaningful work can boost people's engagement and satisfaction.
2. **"Why Small Habits Make a Big Difference" by James Clear** (jamesclear.com) - A detailed exploration of the compound effects of small habits over time.

Tools

1. **Habitica** - An app that gamifies your daily tasks and habits, helping you stay motivated by treating your life like a role-playing game.
2. **Trello** - A versatile project management tool that can track your progress on various tasks and habits.
3. **Evernote** - A note-taking app that can be invaluable for tracking your micro steps and improvements over time.

Podcasts

1. **"The Tim Ferriss Show"** explores world-class performers' daily routines and habits, offering insights that can be applied to using micro steps for personal and professional improvement.
2. **"How to Be Awesome at Your Job"** - This podcast provides tips and tools to improve your work performance, which the micro steps approach can enhance.

Appendix B: A Guide to Tools and Apps That Support the Micro Steps Strategy

Incorporating micro-steps into your daily life requires dedication and the right tools to track and manage your progress. This guide outlines several apps and tools designed to support your micro steps strategy, making it easier to sustain momentum and measure your advancements.

1. Habit Trackers

- **Habitica**: An app that turns your daily goals and habits into a fun game, providing rewards and punishments to help motivate you. Its engaging RPG-style system makes it perfect for those who need extra excitement to stay on track.
- **Streaks**: This app helps you track multiple habits simultaneously, encouraging you to maintain a streak of successful days. Its simple interface is ideal for quick check-ins and updates.

2. Goal Setting and Task Management

- **Trello**: A versatile tool that allows you to create boards and cards to manage tasks and projects. It's excellent for visualizing the steps needed to achieve your goals and tracking progress clearly and organized.
- **Todoist**: Known for its simplicity and effectiveness, Todoist allows you to set up tasks and subtasks, making it easy to break big goals into manageable micro steps. You can track deadlines, prioritize tasks, and celebrate achievements as you complete them.

3. Time Management

- **Forest**: This app helps you stay focused by planting a virtual tree that grows as you work. If you leave the app to

check your phone, the tree dies, promoting focused, uninterrupted work sessions.
- **Focus@Will**: This service provides music scientifically optimized to boost concentration and focus. It is perfect for those who need auditory support to maintain productivity during microtasks.

4. Reflection and Journaling

- **Day One**: A journaling app that makes it easy to record your thoughts, experiences, and reflections on your progress. It's great for keeping a log of your micro steps and the insights you gain along the way.
- **Reflectly**: An AI-driven journal that helps you structure your daily reflections and track your mood, providing insights into how your micro steps impact your overall well-being.

5. Learning and Development

- **Blinkist**: This app provides summaries of non-fiction books, allowing you to quickly grasp key concepts and ideas that can inspire your micro steps in personal development, business, and health.
- **Coursera**: Offers courses on a wide range of topics, many of which can be tackled in small segments. This is ideal for those looking to incorporate educational micro-steps into their routine.

These tools can be tailored to various aspects of your microstep journey, whether maintaining focus, tracking progress, or finding inspiration. Choose the ones that best fit your style and goals and use them as companions for continuous improvement.

Appendix C: Templates and Planners for Tracking Your Micro Steps and Progress

Having the right templates and planners can make a significant difference in effectively implementing and tracking your micro steps. This section provides templates and planners designed to help you organize, track, and reflect on your progress as you apply the micro steps strategy to achieve continuous improvement.

1. Daily Micro Step Planner

A daily planner template is designed to help you outline and track your micro steps each day. This planner lets you specify the micro-step, the expected outcome, and a box to tick once completed. It also includes a section for daily reflections to jot down any insights or adjustments for future micro steps.

2. Weekly Progress Tracker

This weekly tracker template provides an overview of your goals and the micro steps planned for each day of the week. It includes a progress bar for each goal, helping you visualize how close you are to achieving your weekly objectives. There's also space for weekly summaries to reflect on what worked and could be improved.

3. Monthly Achievement Chart

A monthly chart that helps you set long-term micro-step goals and track your monthly progress toward these goals. This template is ideal for more extensive projects or habits that need consistent effort over a longer period. It encourages a monthly review of achievements and areas needing more focus.

4. Habit Formation Worksheet

A worksheet specifically designed for building new habits using the micro steps approach. It guides you through defining the habit, planning the micro steps necessary to establish it, and tracking your consistency and obstacles over time.

5. Project Breakdown Template

For larger goals or projects, this template helps you break them down into actionable micro steps. It includes sections for the goal, the deadline, the list of micro steps, and milestones to celebrate, ensuring you stay motivated and on track.

Daily Micro Step Planner Template

Date: _____

Micro Step Planner

Micro Step	Expected Outcome	Completion
		[ ]
		[ ]
		[ ]
		[ ]
		[ ]

Daily Reflections

- **What went well today?**
    -
    -

- **What could be improved?**
    -
    -

- **Insights for future micro steps:**
    -

"Tiny Triumphs: The Power of Micro Steps in Achieving Continuous Improvement"

Weekly Progress Tracker

Week: _____

Goal Overview:
1. Goal 1: _____
   Progress: [ ][ ][ ][ ][ ][ ][ ][ ][ ][ ] 0% 25% 50% 75% 100%
2. Goal 2: _____
   Progress: [ ][ ][ ][ ][ ][ ][ ][ ][ ][ ] 0% 25% 50% 75% 100%
3. Goal 3:_____
   Progress: [ ][ ][ ][ ][ ][ ][ ][ ][ ][ ] 0% 25% 50% 75% 100%

Daily Micro Steps:
Monday:
   Step 1: _____
   Step 2: _____
   Step 3: _____

Tuesday:
   Step 1: _____
   Step 2: _____
   Step 3: _____

Wednesday:
   Step 1 _____
   Step 2: _____
   Step 3: _____

"Tiny Triumphs: The Power of Micro Steps in Achieving Continuous Improvement"

Thursday:
  Step 1: _____
  Step 2: _____
  Step 3: _____

Friday:
  Step 1: _____
  Step 2: _____
  Step 3: _____

Saturday:
  Step 1: _____
  Step 2: _____
  Step 3: _____

Sunday:
  Step 1: _____
  Step 2: _____
  Step 3: _____

Weekly Summary:
What Worked:

_____

_____

_____

Areas for Improvement:

_____

"Tiny Triumphs: The Power of Micro Steps in Achieving Continuous Improvement"

_____

_____

Additional Notes:

_____

_____

_____

Monthly Achievement Chart

Month: _____

Long-Term Micro Step Goals:
1. Goal 1: _____
   Target Completion Date: _____
   Milestones: _____
      Milestone 1: _____
      Milestone 2: _____
      Milestone 3: _____
   Progress: [ ][ ][ ][ ][ ][ ][ ][ ][ ][ ][ ][ ] 0% 25% 50% 75% 100%

2. Goal 2: _____
   Target Completion Date: _____
   Milestones: _____
      Milestone 1: _____
      Milestone 2: _____
      Milestone 3: _____
   Progress: [ ][ ][ ][ ][ ][ ][ ][ ][ ][ ][ ][ ] 0% 25% 50% 75% 100%

"Tiny Triumphs: The Power of Micro Steps in Achieving Continuous Improvement"

3. Goal 3: _____
   Target Completion Date: _____
   Milestones: _____
      Milestone 1: _____
      Milestone 2: _____
      Milestone 3: _____
   Progress: [ ][ ][ ][ ][ ][ ][ ][ ][ ][ ][ ][ ][ ][ ] 0% 25% 50% 75% 100%

Weekly Breakdown:
Week 1:
   Step 1: _____
   Step 2: _____
   Step 3: _____
Week 2:
   Step 1: _____
   Step 2: _____
   Step 3: _____
Week 3:
   Step 1: _____
   Step 2: _____
   Step 3: _____
Week 4:
   Step 1: _____
   Step 2: _____
   Step 3: _____

Monthly Summary:
Achievements:

_____

_____

"Tiny Triumphs: The Power of Micro Steps in Achieving Continuous Improvement"

Areas for Focus:

_____

_____

_____

Additional Notes:

_____

_____

Habit Formation Worksheet

Habit: _____

Defining the Habit:
Why do I want to build this habit?

_____

_____

_____

What will success look like?

_____

_____

"Tiny Triumphs: The Power of Micro Steps in Achieving Continuous Improvement"

Planning Micro Steps:
1. Micro Step 1: _____

   Frequency: Daily / Weekly / Other: _____
   Expected Outcome: _____
   Start Date: _____

2. Micro Step 2: _____

   Frequency: Daily / Weekly / Other: _____
   Expected Outcome: _____
   Start Date: _____

3. Micro Step 3: _____

   Frequency: Daily / Weekly / Other: _____
   Expected Outcome: _____
   Start Date: _____

Tracking Consistency:
Week 1:
   Day 1: Completed / Not Completed
   Day 2: Completed / Not Completed
   Day 3: Completed / Not Completed
   Day 4: Completed / Not Completed
   Day 5: Completed / Not Completed
   Day 6: Completed / Not Completed
   Day 7: Completed / Not Completed

Week 2:

Day 1: Completed / Not Completed
  Day 2: Completed / Not Completed
  Day 3: Completed / Not Completed
  Day 4: Completed / Not Completed
  Day 5: Completed / Not Completed
  Day 6: Completed / Not Completed
  Day 7: Completed / Not Completed

Week 3:
  Day 1: Completed / Not Completed
  Day 2: Completed / Not Completed
  Day 3: Completed / Not Completed
  Day 4: Completed / Not Completed
  Day 5: Completed / Not Completed
  Day 6: Completed / Not Completed
  Day 7: Completed / Not Completed

Week 4:
  Day 1: Completed / Not Completed
  Day 2: Completed / Not Completed
  Day 3: Completed / Not Completed
  Day 4: Completed / Not Completed
  Day 5: Completed / Not Completed
  Day 6: Completed / Not Completed
  Day 7: Completed / Not Completed

Identifying Obstacles:
  Obstacle 1: _____
  Solution: _____

  Obstacle 2: _____
  Solution: _____

Obstacle 3: _____
Solution: _____

Monthly Reflection:
What worked well?

_____

_____

_____

What can be improved?

_____

_____

_____

Additional Notes:

_____

_____

_____

Project Breakdown Template

Project Title:

_____

"Tiny Triumphs: The Power of Micro Steps in Achieving Continuous Improvement"

Goal:
Overall Goal: _____
 Deadline: _____

Micro Steps:
1. Micro Step 1:
_____
 Due Date: _____
 Notes: _____

2. Micro Step 2:
_____
 Due Date: _____
 Notes: _____

3. Micro Step 3:
_____
 Due Date: _____
 Notes: _____

4. Micro Step 4:
_____
 Due Date: _____
 Notes: _____

5. Micro Step 5:
_____
 Due Date: _____
 Notes: _____

Milestones:
1. Milestone 1:
_____
 Target Date: _____

2. Milestone 2: _____

   Target Date: _____

3. Milestone 3: _____

   Target Date: _____

Progress Tracking:
Week 1:
   Step 1: Completed / Not Completed
   Step 2: Completed / Not Completed
   Step 3: Completed / Not Completed

Week 2:
   Step 1: Completed / Not Completed
   Step 2: Completed / Not Completed
   Step 3: Completed / Not Completed

Week 3:
   Step 1: Completed / Not Completed
   Step 2: Completed / Not Completed
   Step 3: Completed / Not Completed

Week 4:
   Step 1: Completed / Not Completed
   Step 2: Completed / Not Completed
   Step 3: Completed / Not Completed

Monthly Review:
Achievements:

"Tiny Triumphs: The Power of Micro Steps in Achieving Continuous Improvement"

Challenges:

Next Steps:

Additional Notes:

"**Tiny Triumphs: The Power of Micro Steps in Achieving Continuous Improvement**"

www.ingramcontent.com/pod-product-compliance
Lightning Source LLC
Chambersburg PA
CBHW050233230526
45470CB00005B/1927